LION'S GATE

for Carl Rhoden
~ with good wishes
for his own work

Peter Wilson ⊕

March 2, 1989
Gunnison

LION'S GATE

Selected Poems 1963-1986

Keith Wilson

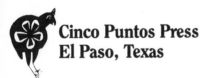
Cinco Puntos Press
El Paso, Texas

ACKNOWLEDGEMENTS

We would like to thank Trask House Books for publishing *Sketches For A New Mexico Hill Town,* Grove Press for *Graves Registry & Other Poems,* Kayak Press for *Homestead,* Sumac Press for *Midwatch,* New Mexico State University for *Old Man & Others: Some Faces For America,* and The Southwestern American Literature Association for *Meeting at Jal.*

Our special thanks go to Utah State University for permitting us to reprint the poems from *While Dancing Feet Shatter The Earth* and *Stone Roses: Poems From Transylvania.* These books are available from the University Press, UMC, Utah State University, Logan, Utah 84322.

**for Heloise
on our 30th Anniversary**

❧ Contents

🐾 Preface to Lion's Gate

It has been many years since I had the initial pleasure of reading poems by Keith Wilson. In the early sixties a magazine called *Wild Dog* introduced me to that careful work. The resonances were unmistakeable and immediately recognizable. They have continued so to the present day. I wrote to Keith at that time. Later, we met, and the man and his poems became one for me. I stress this point. It is not always so, even with those whom we greatly admire. He has made good on his initial promises over a long period of time. The initial intentions have held up. He celebrates his own land, his locus, but he moves—ranges far from that initial pivot solidly in New Mexico to what concerns all of us, what is human, what is inhuman in our abuse of ourselves—war and its consequences. Or he moves far, geographically, to Rumania. Some of his critics have not been able to see him whole, and to realize that these are all facets of the same thing—the same oneness—and a religious celebration in its best sense. A master stone mason knows his stones, and what may not appear cohesive to a casual onlooker, the mason has already related piece by piece and inevitably to a definite design. There are many things that could be said of these poems, of the individual collections represented here, of individual poems, but that will come as a reward to the careful reader, who can then go on and make out the collective shape. It is one poem, no matter how admirable in its many parts—one mastery, and we are all richer for it: *The Selected Poems of Keith Wilson.*

—*Theodore Enslin*

Frontispiece

the vision of this gate:

> granite, stained
> by birds—

Lion's Gate

> which, finally,
> is the stone lion's own
> open mouth, roaring

—is what we pass through

> a taste, a feel:
> the tongue, flame red

—is what passes by

> fangs,
> glistening:
>
> yellow eyes
> that watch

—is an entry, a sort
of gate, passage to, exit
away, the angry maw
roaring

The Lake Above Santos

And there it was, on the banks
of the slow Canadian. A small town,
with people, charged with
the event of their days.

Now the boat passes over,
walls of stone houses clear
beneath the water, windows,
doors, fish swimming thru

      —the sinker pulls my line
down, hook bouncing on a fireplace
the water so translucent one can see
a red coffeepot, homely things.

Below our boat, a whole universe
of fishes, minnows, hurtling
bumping, turning silver,
one great shining ball:

        moving, orbited,
        each one tiny, perfect
        each with his own teeth
        own hunger nudging his belly along.

They pass, a silver globe over
buried houses, conquistador dreams
of ancestors, quiet ghosts of
piñon fires, voices gentle
with evening
speaking

        —under the fingers of the wind
        a thousand minnows
        catch light on tiny scales

Over buried Santos, Hill
Town, a moon rises.

Growing Up

A big Jack, cutting outwards toward blue,
little puffs of my bullets hurrying him.
Sage crushed underfoot, crisp & clean—

My father, a big Irishman, redfaced & watching,
he who could hit anything within range,
who brought a 150-lb. buck three miles
out of the high mountains when he was 57

—a man who counted misses as weaknesses,
   he whipped up his own rifle, stopped the Jack
   folding him in midair, glanced at me, stood
   silent

My father who never knew I shot pips from cards
candleflames out (his own eye) who would've
been shamed by a son who couldn't kill. Riding
beside him.

To My Wife

there are beauties & beauties.
yours are simple, rough
irregular

the boned lines of your face
stand, in certain lights, severe
almost harsh

you worry about seeming old

while I've watched your hands
sewing, seen the strong arcs
they make

      needle passing through
materials drawing firm together
thread lost in weave:

a wholeness, coming together
lost in itself from attention;
we are what we piece together

beauty after beauty the hand
your hand turns in the light, the tuck
is made

there are these beauties & then
there is you, lined fingers following
the silver needle, sewing light
into place

The Rancher

Hard old grey eyes, no pity
in him after years branding cattle—
a cruel man with cows & men

he drove both hard & once
when he was 70 tried to kill
a young puncher for smiling at his

old wife, sat down & cried in fury
because his grown sons took his
ivoryhandled .45 away, held

his head in his arms & didn't
ever come back to the dance.
After awhile his wife went slowly

out into the clear night
saying how late it is getting
now isn't it? without

pity for his eyes, him showing
nothing the next morning
barking at the hands to get

popping, the sun already up,
coffee on the fire & him
stifflegged, hard pot hanging

over the saddlehorn, he led
fall's last drive
across the hazy range.

New Mexico: Campsite Above Bernalillo

                         Shadows blue
going darker slip outward, armies
march, breastplates gleaming
steel
          —by this old river, marching
          toward sea, cottonwood leaves clatter,
          ancient tongues!

          —beyond the cool air of this night
          granite cliffs, the crest of the Sandias rise
          tidal waves of stone, rushing
                            through blue

winds cool out of green spruce & piñon
move past sky—

Beyond the mountains
a new storm shapes, clouds
heavy with moisture, move.

                    2

Out of the silences.   Hawks, coyotes
hunters all with me, moonlit, stalk
these shores

               I lift up my eyes, owls
               circle in pure light, full

moon, it is history walking on soft feet;
sounds, my campfire
before sleep, it is history

shaping itself to stone
the mountains only appear
to move closer as I
breathe

Coyote

here in New Mexico *coyote*
means many things, human
inhuman

               the pretty girl
sitting at my table says
"tu sabes yo soy una coyote"
—half Anglo, half Spanish

an outcast, claimed by none
but her Eastern boyfriend, me,
& my whole family

the split body of one
struck by a car, entrails
bright red-&-white, head
lolling

               that quick shadow
against a moontipped hill,
a god of laughter tracing
his trails through blue blue
hills, his lean nose sniffing
prying

               big bush tails
& thick fur are not for him
—he travels light & far

many of us would walk his trail,
know him, follow his sign to where
it ends, by the northern rim of the sun.

Virginio

—Old Town
Fort Sumner, New Mexico

Separate, lovely with lanterns
this adobe village stood a part
of Spain & laughter, wine,
singing.

old men sat in the sun
talked to children of old days,
of nothing at all. Virginio,
rolling brownpaper *cigarros*,
told stories while a new town
rose beside the Pecos.

Even in 1930 the village
had its gamblers, cockfights,
bailes for quick feet, the dark
silks whirled, glittered in the night,
a laughter of girls, deep voices
of men, followed by a quietness.

we children of the new Anglo town
climbed the road, Virginio becoming
grandfather to us all, Spanish
& Anglo, we sat, ate *tortillas*
in the sun while our fathers worked,
built a world with different
sounds: bulldozers, the clink of cash
in drawers, a measure, worth.

years passed, old walls
no longer slapped with rivermud
in springtime rains, fell. People
moved away, patterns changed,
& Virginio, it is told, screamed,
died, locked in his daughter's
basement

strange memories
mocking him through
a drunken dark, heavy
with children's faces.

Placitas

—for Larry & Lenore

Rising from earth these houses
were old before they were begun:

      yellow straw & river clay
      the silences of grave men
      who dug from the slippery earth
      shaped homes
      & died, leaving them there.

Embraces of friends, mountains
falling about us, the bright heavens
of worlds springing from a handful of glistening
sand. My dark loves I move into, never share,
transient, shapeless loves singing through
bright winds that eat at adobe, kill
mountains.

Woodcarver

Nobody's uncle but mine, he cut
whistles from slippery mountain
birch, carried them home in his
pocket, for me

          —a drunk, he lived
by his wits, an old robber, he stole
books, told lies for bootleg whiskey.

Sitting very straight, frosty, winter-
eyed he stayed in his room, sipped, a
gentleman drunk at noon, calling for
me, shouting my name: and when I
came, he just looked at me, four,
but not ashamed before his eyes.

When he died he filled the longest
casket old John Allen had, plain white.
They stuck a naked pink bulb above the
open lid, for color; they said he
only slept

          Eyes shut, he didn't look
asleep, his pale face, thin fine hair
slicked down, he looked ready to rise
pink light streaming along his beak of
a nose, he looked ready to get up staring,
blue-eyed, the crisp woodchip smell of
him darkening all the roses.

Trio: Billy-The-Kid

what does it now
matter, his name?

song, one of those bloody
marching chants of the Middle
Ages
    —a child's nursery rhyme
    of destruction & love

children singing:

    billy, billy, billy

little girls skipping rope
to gunflashes, boys clutching
their chests, falling
to later rise, eat their suppers
& go sweetly to bed, complete
resurrection

    billy, billy

Bonney (Antrim-McCarty), Bowdre and O'Folliard
rode down the sandy streets of one-horse Mexican towns,
across gullies, their slickers flapping in the rain & wind

    took bright coins for their gunflashes,
paid for cattle the same way, spooked them up draws
and sold them wherever they could, for almost nothing

They had a system and their system was luck,
the goddess of the very young, the brave
and the sick of mind. They rode past *cantina* doorways
hollowing the night with flickering lamps,
past general stores

> (remembering perhaps the one
> where McSween burned to death and the Kid
> fled through the shadows, firing easily
> at any shadow?

Past women, girls singing their soft songs, brushing
bare arms against adobe, waiting. The Kid had girls
everywhere, rode on, his silver conchos bright
—hand always near the gunbutt

> *Colt .38 Lightning Model*
> his gun, an undependable weapon
> with a tricky, easily snapped sear.
> if the sear broke, the gun
> jammed. when it worked, the shots
> lived up to its name, fast as he
> could pull the trigger, a murder
> weapon, not designed for distance
> shooting, a belly gun, for shooting
> bellies—or backs.

Swept on, the three of them, rustling cattle, stealing what
wasn't nailed down, whooping it up, dashing into
small towns, their guns flaming out the night, shouting
like boys at a picnic . . .

He laughed at jails, threw easy smiles: they all report
that. Charming. Of course the two lawmen he shot down
from behind a wall weren't around to testify, nor were
six Indians he killed while they slept in their blankets.
The Colt had its uses. It was fast, and at close range
he didn't miss.

> *billy, billy*

A handsome young man, with strange colorless eyes,
a good smile and hands delicate as a girl's.
Quick and well-trained, ballet dancer of the Colt,
the rope, the dancefloor

billy goat, ram's head
His sex on his saddleseat
& tied to his hip,

billy

ii

In Old Fort Sumner he had a friend, Pete
Maxwell
         (though it was said Pete was simply
        afraid of him, of his habit of firing from the dark,
        his long memory for wrong, other people's of course)

He had a friend, and two more to ride beside him
and shout to the clear New Mexico morning.
He had a girl, later to be seen in the streets
so fat she had to be moved with a wagon
but pretty then. He had money and fame
and fear, which for him was greater than
all of the others. & such fast hands

he killed Joe Grant with those
         tricky fingers, shifted the cylinder
        of a single action so that the hammer
        would fail on the empty chamber used
        as a safety, knowing Joe would try
        to kill him. Joe did try and witnesses
        said Joe looked very surprised when the Kid
        slowly & methodically shot him down

        a legend for you, Billy
        some dreams that rise
        out of the blood's singing,
        needs that come with the bones,
        breath, other limitations

        billy, billy, o billy

iii

no-name, no-name
yah, yah!
he's got no
na-ame!

the children play on,
& cock their guns
at shadows, hide in
their shallow, cool caves
pretending outlaw lairs
& posses

Pat Garrett trapped the Kid at Stinking Springs,
surrounded the cabin with his men, fired until
they killed O'Folliard. Bowdre, gunned down later
as he and the Kid rode into Fort Sumner.
The Kid whirled his horse, rode away fast,
leaving his last buddy in the dust.

They got him later, of course. Everyone knows
that—how he walked in from his sweetheart's shack,
went onto Pete Maxwell's porch to cut a piece
of fresh meat from the beef hanging there to cure.

He heard voices, paused, knife in hand, asked
"¿Quién es?" & Pat Garrett, hidden behind
Pete Maxwell's bed, fired at the shadowed youth
filling the doorway. He fell.

In the shocked quiet, Garrett said, "Is it
him?" & waited. Finally the Mexicans gathered
around, turned the body over. *"Si, Señor. Es*
El Chivato." And then the speaker cried, for the Kid
was good to them, did not kill them, and let them feel
he was like them, though he was not, and they knew it.
He was powerful though, and while he himself was a Gringo,
he spoke good Spanish, and he killed Gringos. They loved

14

him, let him take their women and their homes and their
hearts and still in that Valley it is hard to find
anyone to speak a bad word in Spanish about El Chivato,
the little goat, who they say was not buried in that
abandoned military cemetery at all but who rode on
& now walks the road by moonlight waiting for his people
to call him, El Chivato, the kid with the tricky,
tricky hands, the colorless eyes

        o, billy

        riding your thousand horses
        kissing your girls, drowned
        in the timed blood of your
        hoofbeats, the perfectly flat
        prairies, llano estacado, wave
        their grasses

        children's eyes
        caught to the hereditary madness
        of spilled blood and a glory
        that dries on the hands, echo
        your name, the quick explosions
        of years, dust blowing by
        your grave & up the Valley

        billy, billy, billy

The Touch Of Moonlight

My male ancestors
prowled this land
like heavy mountain
cats spewing their
hatred & their life
dropping spoor, flicking
tail, a howl in their chests
for the darkness, the chipped
winds of the highroad valleys

—my dad was tailed by
a puma all the way back
from some girl's house. He
forgets her name but he went
back the next night, quick
—shadowed as any cat, its
cries like a woman's cries
breaking through the shafts
of moonlight

I walk the high thin
fences, domesticated,
dig my claws in rotten
wood & feel my belly
rock from side to side
as the door opens, yellow
street light! and out
into a night crisp with
exhaust smoke & pretence

I am a fatcat and walk
the slender fences of a city
remembering woods

          the touch
of moonlight on my eyes, the
touch of moonlight

Teófilo's Father

died on the Cross at Easter.
a Penitente, chosen.
brought in his young manhood
to the *morada* & beaten:
the Wounds of Christ, one
by one they pierced him.

He marched in the procession.
Men, carrying whips, lashed him
& each other up the rocky hill.
They tied him on the Cross, raised
it, tamped the dark earth firm.

Later, after vigil, they cut
him down, his lips pale, head
hung down, his loincloth red
from the knifeslash in his side.

Brothers carried him in honor
through the streets of our village:
for three days they sang & marched,
bearing the corpse until the smell
drove all but the devout away.

Finally, my father, his friend,
put the tarpwrapped body
in his pickup, drove it
all the way to Anton Chico

—The brown dead Christ, jogging
   in the truck, while ahead
   the Brothers waited, knowing somehow
   He was coming, throwing their
   chants & offerings into silver
   moonlight, dust from the pickup
   rising like incense around the
   proud, stern figures.

17

The Mistress Of My Father

Grim (to my eyes), soft
to memory, the pale blue dress
blond hair

wisps catching in the breeze.
Her long thin hands, uneasy
eyes made me uncertainly
welcome

          I, presumed too young
to know relationships. Aware,
yet unable to act, unsure before
warmth, longing for the approval
of my father's eyes, not her's, I
stood in the summer's sunshine, orphaned
by the huge distance between,
their closing bodies

Santa Ana House

where we leased from Indians,
Heloise (part Choctaw), I,
born of this Indian State.

—its flagstoned walls
rose to gleaming *vigas,*
a huge main room bristled
in firelight

          & outside
shadows, low hills, the moon
struck out a history, a *campo
santo* of ghosts, old battles

          (In the 1600's two fights
between the Spaniards & Isletas
happened here & even older burial
grounds ring these hills)

          —where the two of us,
newly married, walked among
dead eyes, the sharper points
of the night, hatreds from
the past

          & saw the moon
silver the hills, toward Placitas
it glistened on the river

          old Masks moving
around the house, as we slept
Kachinas slipped forward, terrible
rattles

          in the night the moon
blazed cold with silver; the rock
named "Serpent's Head" lay a mile
away; recent prayer sticks there,
eagle feathers fluttering

          —this solid house
where we held each other, sure in
the love we brought, a respect for
those gods, we caught ourselves in
similar rituals, dualities of
earth spinning beneath our bed
a vision of brightness, old dreams
to guard us darkly, darkly through
the reaches of an ancient night.

Teófilo Orozco

who was just my size, my friend
with whom I fought & played;
who had a dog much like mine.

Hunting together, we walked
winter mesas for rabbits,
our guns alike, easy in our
hands the silver light of them
caught in the frost. Rimrocks
surrounded us, blue & cold.

Later, after the Army, the Navy,
we met, spoke uneasily & as I shook
his hand I saw the blue tattooed cross,
the slashed rays of the Pachuco, man
of violence, hater of Gringos.

His hand slipped away, he
nodded—Spanish to Anglo—
and walked stiffly back
to his watching friends, their
dark eyes upon us, the street
closing on alien faces.

Snakeskin

—for Vance Wilson

Today my daughter called to me:
"A snake! A snake!" and there on the road,
in his green-sheened loveliness

he writhed, back broken
his delicate head turning
gracefully with his pain

his minutes slipping by him
on the hot asphalt road.

It was of course coincidence
that, the same morning, I heard
of my grim old uncle's death

"Pull over," he said to his wife,
"I don't think I'm going to make it."
He died beside the road,

& I swear the world will never be
as full again even though the hailstorm
that came that afternoon crackled & rustled
& slashed through the coiling dark sky.

Old Man

       of the hills moon
caught like a buckle
on your back, your lean dog
at your side

       the valleys are gold
tonight, the coyote's hunting
song a warm robe to wrap around
your thin shoulders

       with just enough stars
to keep your eyes warm

The Old Man & His Calf

. . . that he'll never sell, though
he bought it for market. Each
day, he postpones the day, the calf
grown to bull, he yanks and tugs
him down the meadow, cursing
affectionately, buying more
and more feed

       it is the same with
the five chickens, and the goat
called Eleanor who ate his only
hat . . . "One of these days!"
he says

       and eats his saltpork beans
with a rusty spoon, the whole bunch
of animals, fat, grazing, pecking
peacefully all around his shack.

The Old Man And His Snake

The two lived there, almost together;
he in the shack, the snake below under
the warped boards in the cool darkness
cut by rays of light from the lamp above.

A thick Diamondback, nearly six feet long,
it moved out in moonlight to stalk rabbits
and rats. Out his window the old man pointed:
"There he goes, not enough to feed him around
here nomore. Haven't had a rat or a mouse
in near two years. *He's* the reason. Old
Snake!"

      The two of them, growing old, keeping
careful distances from each other, geographies
of agreement (the old man stayed in at night,
the snake never went out in the day . . .)

The old man pointed to his chamberpot. "Bought
that to keep from tangling with him. Can't use
the outhouse at night. Kill him? Why the hell
do that? He's got a right to live, ain't he?
Besides, I always know he's there, down under
the boards, hear him move every once in awhile.
A man needs something to keep him company
and there's worse critters than snakes
lots worse than snakes. . . ."

The Drug Store

In the early evenings the families came
sat, drinking cokes outside and listened
to the radio or talked. A meeting place,
news got passed, advice sought.

> one night, a fat old man
> while teasing a baby
> tossed him high
> into the smokefilled
> air inside & the great
> fan cut the boy's
> head off.

> the man caught
> the trunk
> & carried it to
> its mother

The Old Man At Twilight

. . . gets caught

> looking across the darkening
grasses, the sun's shadows move along the land,
touch his face. Once he said, thinking of an
old song, that he sometimes saw the sons he
never had at twilight, sometimes he thought
he saw them walking kneedeep in shadows
toward him.

Standing there, his muscles
loose, face sagging just a little, eyes
focused out beyond the Hill, it's how we
remembered him best, the work done, dinner
on the stove, the tatter of old masks
clinging to his face

—*for Tom Rose*

The Gift

—*for my daughter Kathleen*

This is a song
about the gift of patience

of opening

the need to walk alone
ever, deeper, into

This is a poem
against light

a recommendation
to darkness

Bring a candle
the room is warm

This is a song

The Voices Of My Desert

Beginning this new trail, with the resonance
of shifting earth about me, I hear calls
distancing the crow voices of my childhood,

the wolf cry of my middle age. The sun
is an ancient symbol above me and God knows
what the mountains, spirit blue on the horizon

mean. Silence stands within me as without
desert stirs to its own subtle communication.
There is time, always, to wonder, doubt.

New Mexico is a myth, an ancient whirlpool
of time where moments stand still just before
being sucked down to other planes, other hours.

We hold time back through rituals, dances
that stir the seconds like flecks of sand
beneath our feet, eternities of the possible.

I write down the words I hear, but I know
it is the Dead who speak them. Our ears
are tuned to the past, hear, hear the days

less clearly than the flute-songed nights
with their last owls whitefaced as moons
swooping low for the poisoned, dying mice.

The ghosts of wolves ring our hills.
Those birdcries, Comanche songs drifting
up from wartrails; the click of steel

in the night, prospectors or old soldiers
sharpening the edge of darkness to a keen
wind that blows all the stories away.

26

The Wolf Tryptych

The Morning of the Wolf

The first time I saw him, he rose
out of the grass of a hill, his eyes
straight into mine, big head low

He moved toward me, ignoring the man
who stood beside me with the gun, his eyes
straight into mine. I was thirteen,
taught to hate and fear wolves. He, a *lobo*,
a Mexican wolf from below the border.
His eyes. I keep coming back to that.
The way they bore the center of me.

The gun began firing wildly, bullets
splashing dust around the wolf but he
hardly moved, his eyes never left mine
until I broke the contact and saw the man
his hands shaking, spraying the .22 bullets,
caught completely in buck fever, the wolf
almost laughing, eased off through the grass
his tail a contemptuous banner

—his every movement sure of the morning, me,
the long years I would remember his yellow eyes
that big head looking at me

        I recall the smell of sage
and creosote, the fear of that man, courage
of the wolf. Held in my brain, he never
went away at all. His footsteps sound outside
my city window. His cry rises and falls
on the dawn wind.

The Day of the Wolf

The other ranchers came this morning,
early; in the crisp blue air of Fall
they stood stiffly—each holding his reins
his restless horse, took coffee, nodding
a "thank-you-mam," his rifle hanging
beside him in a scratched leather
scabbard

        —the wolf was back, three calves
slaughtered yesterday, their white faces flat
on the ground, big eyes splattered with dirt

:Wolf, running free past the traps in search
of fresh meat, he couldn't be fooled by bait.

That evening we got him just the same,
shot him down when he came to smell
the bitch coyote we'd staked out,
got him, horses in a circle he
couldn't cross, but he fought well,
stood his ground, slugs slapping
him down, him getting up, snarling
showing his teeth until he died.

The horses wouldn't carry his hide
back and we left it there, bloody in the
dusk, his skinny body white as a child's
in the waving tall grass.

The Night of the Wolf

A day, an hour, and it's gone, those years
when fences were rare, game everywhere: New
Mexico

      His wolf face looking at me
that hillside in a childhood sun
the fear and fascination of his eyes how
I saw them then, changing, the flecked
yellows, silvered fur, long blunt muzzle
his quick feet and confidence

They killed him, as he killed,
but they didn't eat him.
He would have eaten them.

He's back. I saw him last night.
He came to talk to me I think,
to tell me of the ruin of this land
(he wouldn't know how sick I am with it)
He didn't say anything of course,
what do wolves say?
He only looked at me, his eyes
full of concern and then he trotted off.

The game's gone and, I guess, we're going
to go with it. Predators need game, they
can't live without it. That wolf and I
are brothers, or why would he have come,
why warn me unless he thought I could do
something about it. I can't, I guess he
saw that, us both remembering that childish
hillside with its sun, him running so free,
rabbits popping up everywhere like furry flowers.

Hill Man

—Albuquerque, New Mexico

First he and his wife lived here
with their Spanish daughter
& stunted Indian-Spanish
son-in-law.

Then she died and he, tall,
whip-hard, stood alone in the neat yard
his new clothes too big for him
choosing not to see suburbs surrounding him.

—Staring toward the high, pale mountains
of his manhood, where his wife and he
tended sheep in the blue air. . . .

Once he took my blonde baby
held her in his arms and said
"Qué linda tu eres, Chica." Gently.
He drew the sign of the Cross
on her soft forehead, for witches,
he said, were everywhere, still watch
from the mountains and would curse
a beautiful child praised
and without protection.

30

Old Women
Beside A
Church

the blackshawled women of New Mexico
wait, wait outside their churches, in the
gusty winds, their black dresses

in frail silk & gauze they wait, widows
of Christ, faces stiffly furrowed

cracked to mud they watch, eyes centered
deep in the

      clanging bell

enter
burn candles for a soul, for
cold beds, flickering oil lights
the wind brushes adobe walls away
grain by grain

Twin Aces

back to back, Stud poker & an open
pot. The play, intense, grew harder.
Clark, Bowers, McMorris & my dad, cool
professionals: "Poker's for men," my dad'd
say, paying out his debts with grocery money,
bringing his tales with flushed face to our
quiet home. Great stories from the tall
fierce combats he lived for

     while I, a comrade,
a spy posted by mother, sat by propping
my eyes open & pleasing father who thought
at last I'd shown a normal interest.

     Thick cigar smoke
& the sharp smell of whiskey, I remember
that, & the naked bulb, those men
flicking cards into the pot of light
slitted eyes watching their fall
as if it were their own:

     yet my father won
with a slipped ace & we got out quick
before the discards were counted. Walking
home, 4 a.m., my father singing & looking
back over his shoulder, the quiet street
behind him.

—for Richard Russell

New Mexico: Paso Por Aquí

. . . that which none other
would occupy.
—Arthur Conan Doyle

Such might be said of this land
by those whose eyes fill to trees,
light buds caught in gentler winds.

These sweeps of sandstone, lava, cracked
mountains holding in themselves darkness,
great canyons

        buzzards flapping
against stiff winds, golden scorpions
high, clear skies
—old gods that look down
their turquoise eyes
glittering

This is an old land, dry & brittle.
Its charms are bones, hollowed to whistles,
dancing feet hidden by rising dust.

Here, we live uneasily, aware the sun
has stripped us, we know our bones
our dry flesh that whispers as we walk.

The skull of a cow
pared to a white clarity.
Snake, coiled in the rocks
his rattle another whisper, a reminder
that we are not alone, do not
alone own this land, nor walk
upon it too freely. It is held
the Indians used to say, by God.
All men are visitors here.

The Name-Giver

Driving through the Sacramento Mountains
three in the morning of a spring day.
Mountains of the Holy Sacraments, slender
pines whipping by in late starlight.

I had been driving since ten that morning.
Now, fighting sleep, unable to stop
because of the twisting narrow road
I listened to my Turtle daughter beside me
telling me her kind of jokes, her histories
of fabled animals—Keeping Daddy Awake
was what she later called it all.

I glanced out the window and running beside
the car in the crisp light was a naked man
with the head and eyes of a wolf. I saw his
firm trunk, the light fur over his chest
and stomach, the heavy bush and long penis
that swung between his thighs as he ran.

He was grinning and looking at me.
I thought of mentioning it to Turtle but
what if she didn't see him, I thought, how
would she handle that? Me seeing someone she
didn't. For a moment, I tried to pretend
he wasn't there, glanced back and sure enough
he was keeping up, effortlessly, looking at me
and smiling with his fine white teeth.

Something passed between us, I can't say what,
some look from our eyes, and just as the thought
began to enter my head that, wolf face or not,
he looked a lot like a younger me, he waved his
hand in salute and raced off into the darkness
of the pine trees.

My mind clear, I found a spot
soon and parked but couldn't sleep, sensing his form
moving through the brush, watsching and guarding us.

An Indian would have said I had my name when I
awoke the sun and faint circle of the moon
were paintings on an old hide, carefully tanned
and held by chiefs against whatever darkness
of memeory or charm might come to the tribe, the
children singing, Heloise driving now,
counting the miles to our house, its solid doors.

Yellow Green

are the colors of this land, if you add
brown, and blue for the sky, black
for the nights.

       I was opening or shutting
a barbed wire gate, walked around the car
to get in and saw his eyes, round, dark
watching me

       For a second I thought
he was a gopher snake, harmless . . . I'd raised
one for a year, became as much a friend
as a snake will permit, liked him deeply
and hated to turn him loose, to live
where he must, I where I must. . . .

Then he raised his viper's head and my eyes
traveled along his yellowish green smoothness
to where the rattles stood erect, quivering.

I could not hear them, but that is another
story coming out of the crash of gunfire
that surrounded my young manhood. For a second
I felt tightness, I knew him, Old Enemy
respected by the Indians and my father as wise,
fierce, uncompromising
                              I knew our brotherhood.
I stretched out my hand. He didn't coil
nor did he relax and I squatted down just out
of striking distance. We talked. I tried
to explain how he must move from the road,
I would not hurt him. He seemed to understand,
the quiver of his rattles lessened, his head
lowered but he was uncertain, afraid, uneasy
of turning his back to me, a man.

I couldn't blame him. I too trust snakes more
than most men, believe them in their quick honesty.

Finally I threw some small clods near his head
so that he could see I was capable of hurting him
but chose not to . . . a logic wild creatures understand.

He crawled away, his beautiful body vivid in afternoon
sun, rattles still and my hand unconsciously reached
farther out to him.
                              I, wishing I could follow and join
with his warm world of hunting and loving, tie myself
into a ball with him and his sisters and brothers, sleep
the long winter through, dreaming of rabbits and mice,
the sweet rites of spring

A rancher killed a snake the next morning.
He said it looked a lot like my friend.

The colors of this land are blood & bone.

In Sere & Twisted Trees

—El Rito, New Mexico

Walking the small trails of stonecropped hills,
my son and I read with the grains of our skins
the old language, its tongues of night and day,
toned winds and the watching trees and skies.

How it all grows easy and secure when one realizes
everything is alive in the summer's sun, listening
watching. I speak to my brothers. I tell them
we are coming, meaning no harm. Wait. My son, 10,
is a fisherman, and he hopes to catch trout.
I tell them this, promise he will eat what he catches.
I will see to this.

                    A prayer for the trout.
A prayer for my son, whom I love more than ever
watching his graceful figure dance to the rod
and fly he made. I needn't have bothered the trout.
He was wiser than my son. We walk back, Kevin,
still excited, apparently not caring about the lack
of fish, full of the adventure of the day.

He no longer holds my hand now, and I understand.
His embraces are quick, embarrassed, his eyes
shifting warily away towards the hills. It won't
be long, as this canyon's time is measured,
before he leaves me. Pray for me, Trout.
Pray for me, Mountain Stream.

The Arrival Of My Mother

—New Mexico Territory, 1906

She got off, according to her diary,
dressed in a lovely beaded gown, fresh
from Washington with sixteen trunks of ballgowns,
chemises, blouses (4 Middle), shoes and assorted
lingerie. She was at that time about 25, old
for an unmarried woman. Her stiff mother was at
her side, she also wildly overdressed for New Mexico
sun and wind.

What must she have thought, seeing my uncle standing,
hat in hand in the dust of that lonely train house,
cracked yellow paint, faded letters of welcome
for passengers that rarely come?

The buckboard was waiting and they rode out into
the darkness of evening toward the tent, that half
built frame homestead house, wind dying as the sun
sank, birdcries stilled.

I see her now outshooting my father and me, laughing
at our pride and embarrassment. My sister, as good a
shot, waiting her turn. Or that picture of her
on horseback, in Eastern riding clothes beside the Pecos.
A picnic when I was small and how my father lifted me up
to her and she carefully walked the horse around rock
and sand.

I suppose she finally arrived in New Mexico
in the April of one year when my sister and I sat beside
a rented bed, each holding one of her hands and watched
her eyes grow childlike, unmasked as a *kachina*
entering the final *kiva* of this Dance. The graceful
the slim laughing woman of my childhood. The old mother
heavy with years slipped away and the woods of New
England dimmed as these dry hills ripened and caught
her last breath, drums, drums should have sounded
for the arrival of my mother.

Vision

We sat, you and I,
upon a bridge and watched
dry sand blow by.

Nothing in that.
Sand, and a view of change,
rough wind upon our skins.

To love the desert marks
one, leaves him both alone
and claims him, your hand

slips into mine the way
the sun glides down
to sudden night, the fierce

desert nights of owl
and swift snake. Moon
white as the wind dies

your face drives the night
the small clouds of evening
darken now about your hand.

To My Daughters

Children, walking or playing in the sun or
bright behind low clouds; children dancing
out old rituals all but they forget:

>Lady O, Lady
>O turn around;
>
>Lady O, Lady
>O, touch the
>
>ground, O my
>darlings

skipping to the circling arc of ropes, the
brightness can be lost, daughters who make a man's
house a place of singing—daughters skipping &
out, too, is a way of breaking free before sun.

—for Roxanne, Kathleen, Kristin, and Kerrin

Day Of The Pig

—Sacramento Mountains, 1940

one of them, grazing the still
meadow, slightly behind the others.
a man in our hunting party who wished
despite warnings "to have fresh pig
for supper"

    spotted domestics
gone wild, they were taller, heavier
than javelinas, meaner
my father said

    be ready to run
but there wasn't time, the fool
missed & the pregnant young sow, black spotted
white in the early dusk, charged
faster than I ever knew a pig could run,
low, the pounding of her sharp hooves

    & I dropped to one knee, opened
fire: saw dust fly from .22 hits,
head on, pig coming, dust,
an angry snapping of teeth

until his 30/30 slug caught her flush
& spun her down, blood trickling
from her relaxing snout

we cut her open, keeping an eye
to the rest of the sounder, dressed
her & later, beside a mesquite wood fire
the man ate shining piglets
one after the other, saying
how delicious they were, smacked
his lips and laughed, sun already
down—a clear moon lighting
the still mesa.

41

The Old Flyer

Double-spanning wings, biplane
struts & wires howling
out of the sun
diving

        & the marriage photograph:
        a slim young officer with
        wings, a silver blur
        on the old print.

            She, dark
        crazed eyes, off to one
        side, slightly cowering.

Darkness splits, the echoes
of machineguns behind, crosses
fall lazily
trailing flames

        She, running, screaming
        in the night, hides under
        her mother's bed, sobbing
        still in her bridal gown.

On the wall, a propellor.
German. Splintered at
one tip. Carefully
varnished, glistening.

        —What had they all to do, a Spad
        circling in high light, the
        guns & later, the handsome face
        (no death hides in the eyes of
        the photo, the bride
        never returns

What had any thing to do
with this fat old man behind
the beer, smiling into the
night, tapping his fingers?

The Politicians

                come
come here with full bellies
& shined shoes to the one street
of San Miguel, talking, waving
hands, their harsh gringo Spanish
shouted in the hanging dust
of the square

     the men of the town
stand uneasy, aware of their hard
hands, the blue of the stranger's
eyes, their own mudcrusted boots
stiff with clay

they are ashamed these men
whose hands are strong with work & loving.
they listen. then go to the bar,
beer & red wine, jukebox Infante songs,
his dead voice singing of a Mexico
which was sad, beautiful, but theirs
—riding free across a green land,
gritos on their lips & dead politicians
fall, one-by-one before their dreaming guns.

Echoes, Seafalls For Heloise

i

graceful birds, tall yet distant ships
with lateen sails blazing white, sailing
outward before rays of setting gunfire, far
battles: it is they I speak of, touch here.

A woman, newborn, beckons from the waves,
beckons, Lady, from the foam, breasts like suns,
watergleaming emeralds in her hair: it is she
I speak of, turning her voice towards spray,
shining in, tideborne.

ii

my darling
no bird of the sea touches more gently
than you; far away, the lanterns of war
ships hulled down twinkle, sea winds crying
my name, as you do, racing, long legs flying
through our yard—laughing, your yellow hair
a battle pennant before the sun, streaming . . .

victory over sea
coming later as love, a home safe from waves; challenge,
is a singing in the wind, a crashing

A Birthday Poem For Diana Hadley

Being,
        in the smaller senses
                —flowers
                   girls

are distinctly touches,
movements within the air
perceiving, enveloping
them, what they are

       IS

slender stalks, opening
blossoms

       a green-ness
a texture the *eye*
takes on the way skin
accepts breezes
sharp points of branches

       —as I said
the touches, some girls,
they brush like flowers
against men.

from Graves Registry

GRAVES REGISTRATION: A Joint-Service Operation that comes in after battles, & wars, to count the dead, identify bones, draw up a total of what has been lost . . .

Aus dunklem Wein und Tausend Rosen rinnt die Stunde rauschend in den Traum der Nacht.

> Note: All German quotations are to be found in
> *The Lay of the Love and Death of Coronet*
> *Christopher Rilke* by Rainer Maria Rilke.

Korea—Japan, 1950–53

I

> . . . *Wein, leuchtend*
> *in eisernen Hauben. Wein? Oder*
> *Blut?—Wer kanns unterscheiden?*

Some thing is coming.

a significance, growing, emerges
from the deep green water, slick
with oil. At first it shows a low shape,
resembles a shark, or a killer whale:

> long & dark, with fins.

Nearer the surface, a glow of blue,
a gleam from the cockpit, sense
of someone within—a paleness
viewed through uncertain light.

The increasing apprehension, uneasy
excitement.

It's free. The cables of the straining crane
draw taut & the water opens, parts with suction
& gurgles

    —the plane, wings shorn off, body
     intact, is lifted, gleaming, blue,
     paint freshly wet into the bright
     sun of Tokyo Bay.

Pilot & gunner sit stiff
in their proper places; radioman
below, can't be seen, the awareness
of him alone is there

     each has his goggles set, heads
     leaning slightly forward against
     the restraining straps. Lenses
     wink dully.

Then in the vanishing water
in the bright air flesh slides off long dead
skulls, the helmets shrink & collapse
out of sight as the hook drops the TBM, looking
almost new, on the waiting barge.

     NB: an autopsy revealed
       the pilot was killed
       by one piece of shrapnel
       which neatly severed
       each vertebra in turn.
       the gunner & the radioman
       were alive when the plane
       hit the water.

IV

Und bebende Trommeln.

the captain:

Army of the United States. About 40,
small, lean. Colt .32 Auto
snug under his armpit, the kind eyes
of somebody's uncle.

His men: tall for Koreans, all
carried M-1's (because there, big men
have big rifles, it is the custom

& what happened to his eyes
the changes when he spoke of their raids
of villages flaming, women & children
machinegunned as they ran
screaming from their huts:

> his own sense of the stillness
> (which he told of) as the Gray
> Marine engines caught & they
> drew away, leaving the bodies
> in their white clothes
> sprawled here & there, big
> & small, blood seeping into
> white, junks slipping
> smoothly away

V

. . . ganz in Waffen

Along the coast heavy clouds of dawn
bucked and heaved, arteries of flame pulsed,
subsided

       aboard ship, signal flags
    popped in the wind
& slowly the amphibious squadron took station;
the flagship, dead center of the formation,
moved slowly, then faster

      quiet intensified.
   no one spoke, the ship scuttled
   its 11 knots across a passive sea

         Gunflashes grew vivid now
but still they heard only the engines of the ship,
the wind. A cruiser, lying off a small island
rocked, fired in heavy salvos

     their LST followed
   the breeze-whipped Flag
   straight for the beach
   & the guns . . .

He'd been watching his face,
speaking to him occasionally,
sensing the recruited strength.
The boy rarely answered.

The guns could be heard now. Low, distant.
Heavy 8" whooms! lighter 5's, auto 3's
from the cruiser. A few destroyers also
popped away when suddenly a round from the beach
burst off the bow into a
yellow flower

    the kid broke, no real danger
   but he broke. It was in
   his eyes, in terror
   he edged for the hatch

The officer stopped him with his voice. Quick, flat.
The boy looked about ten standing there, the wind
from the open bridge tugging his hair.
Come back here, he said. The boy did.
Stand here by me, he ordered. He did, close.
They went through the action that way, & neither
was afraid.

VI

(Korea, 1952)

guerilla camp

We arrived at Sok To
before dawn, caught the last
of the tide & slipped the LST's bow
high on the beach.

> he was waiting, bent
> slightly over, hiding
> his hand. he didn't
> wave.

Later, after a good breakfast
aboard, an Army captain took
us on a tour of the guerilla
camp:

> & he followed, tagged
> along like somebody's
> dog. a tall Korean,
> patient.

We were shown the kitchens, & the
tent barracks, the specially built
junks with their concealed engines

& he watched, never
leaving us with his
eyes

Through the hospital, saw four
sheetcovered bodies from the
raid the night before, didn't
ask whose men they were, spoke
kindly to the wounded & gave
them cigarettes

until he strode up,
stuck his shattered hand
in my face, anger & hatred
flaming in his eyes &
shouted & shouted & shouted

waving that hand, the
bones crumpled by
a rifle slug & pushed
almost through the skin,
hardened into a glistening
knot

He was one of ours, a retired fighter,
about my age, my height. They told me
he wanted to know how a man
could farm
with a hand like that.

VII

the singer

who did sing, whose voice
spoke out of a guitar's darkness;
in a clear young night he
sang midwatches away, telling
of country lands, of growing crops,
green corn, tall in the fields

of Kentucky; dark songs of loves,
concerns and ancient questions
he had not yet lived to confirm
or deny.

17. About 6'1". Heavyset,
with plowman's hands & walk.
Then there was my gun.
In its way, it sang too. Clean machine
oiled & perfect, the slide flashed
back over my relaxed hand pow. pow. pow.
& .45 wadcutter slugs crimped neat holes
in the fluttering paper; the gun
was a happiness to my hand.

Many nights that boy was the whole
watch as I would lean against the flying
bridge, coffee growing cold in my cup,
listening to that voice singing out
the darkness ahead.

Then came the time in port. Just before
the invasion. The gunners mates were
cleaning all weapons for the coming action &
claimed mine too.

I was on the bridge
checking the charts. An indistinct
popping sound. Silence.
Running feet, & shouts.

When I got back to the fantail
he was lying there, his boy's face
twisted & gray, big farmer's hands
held in his guts, guitar beside him.

My gun in the destroyed gunner mate's hand.
Smoking faintly.
These are the things that get lost.
Guitars. Guns. Hands to hold
onto them.

X

"Bist Du die Nacht?"

the girl,

in an Inchon officer's club,
small breasts, thin indirect face
but with a silk gown, marks of rank
about her

& how easily she came
later, in the dark, the lips parted
Korean words in passion in light
not understood

the crinkle of paper,
passing hands

XI

guns

chattering guns, bright flames
about their mouths, talking an old
tongue through

their beauty gets forgotten

the quick rush of a kind of singing
moving toward to gunfire to death which
asks nothing but fearlessness
crazy shouts

dying men, in their breathing,
to leave curious legends
terror
pieces of rusted metal

XIV

sea songs for women

"To Those We Leave Behind"
—Old Navy Toast

such power, recorded, is the trace
of days, bright promises of what
could have been

        dreams
dreams of young blood, girls
shining & clean in the sunshine
of springtime beaches

crinkling hair & the endless, forever
repeated words, out of a common pulse,
speaking of the love's concerns:

        bright moon, rising
        as it did, over Sumeria,
        over Mu, over the cracked
        terraces of drowned Atlantis

—Sisters, companions, died in
locked arms, time time again
turned upon the words spoken
half-remembered, memory of the
pale lady rising out of foam

        gesturing, the clean
        drive of cycles turning

love, speaking like guitars
a singing that drives the night
around us like a robe.

XV

the mistress

and there was Akiko.
her child's face, her hatred
of all Americans, save one:

whom he held in his arms,
Akiko. vision of a dead brother
blown to pieces in front of her
his brains on her dress.

he, four. she, ten.

Akiko, who was ashamed
not of loving but of
forgetting

while his own dead
floated the Yellow Sea
burned slowly in planes
died gasping, jagged holes
in their chests

they held each other
through horrors higher
than language, built

a brightness to curtain
the blue, newly made cannon
nightmare bombs stamped "U.S.A."

> *Und da schämt er sich fur sein weisses Kleid.*
> *Und mochte weit und allein und in Waffen sein.*
> *Ganz in Waffen.*

XVI
December, 1952

Back to the combat zone.

Ships, exactly stationed, at darkness
their wakes catch white fire, long graceful lines
blue stacksmoke, fading to night

red battle lamps, men walking
ghosts in the chain lockers
old chanties sung in the small watches
of morning

Nelson, battle signals snapping,
coming about, broadside ready

Farragut, headed in . . .
the shores blazing with light
exploding shells a terror,
the clam voice on the bridge

Skeleton crews, prize ships,
returning to Ur of the Chaldees, swords raised
gleaming before the dying sun

A blue United Nations patch on the arm, a new
dream. One Word. One
Nation.

Peace.

The old bangles, dangled
once more, always working,
buying allegiances

                    stabbing
            tracers hit a village,
            the screams of women, children
            men die

It is when the bodies are counted
man sees the cost of lies, tricks
that blind the eyes of the young. *Freedom.*
Death. *A life safe for.* The Dead.

Casualties are statistics
for a rising New York Stock Market—
its ticker tapes hail the darkeyed
survivors, and cash registers
click, all over the nation, these men
deceive themselves. War is for. The Dead.

XX

hiroshima. hiro-
shima. hi-ro-shi-ma.

I, an American, try
to say that word, to
pronounce it like
my Japanese girl, turning
my tongue on it
as its own streets
turned & twisted,
radiating outward

—to speak, through
this sign, what
it is to be american,
japanese in a century
of terror

        my face it
shapes itself to tongue;
her eyes gleam back, mirrored,
I speak the word & see
—oval eyes, a burned cheek,
trace the scars
with shaking fingers

XXI

commentary

After the raid, the bodies
are lined on the beach. We can
see them across the way, the living
standing beside them in their white
robes, the wind hitting in gusts
across the separating bay

that these men died
that our guerillas shot them
down in a darkness
is perhaps not so important.

God kills, they say
justifying man's ways
to those patterns they
see surround them

deaths. lists of victims
in a language the uncle
back home couldn't read
if he saw it, whose enemies
are always faceless, numbers
in a paper blowing in the
Stateside wind.

How many bodies would
fill a room
living room with TV, soft
chairs & the hiss
of opened beer?

We have killed more.
The children's bodies alone,
would suffice.

The women, their admittedly
brown faces frozen in the agony
of steel buried in their stomachs,
they too would be enough

but aren't, are
finally not piled high enough
the cost of war must be paid, bullets
made for firing, fired. O,
do not dream of peace while such bodies
line the beaches & dead men float
the seas, waving, their hands
beckoning
   rot, white bones
  settle on yellow bottom mud.

XXII

truce

Now the pace changes.
Ships come home, cruisers
their stacks still, blow
no more blue trails over the sea . . .

Truce.

& no more green
wakes, swirling white
bubbles shining
blades, turning

Uniforms in mothballs,
gold braid tarnishing,
ribbons stuck with stars,
faded emblems.

The Flag, dreams.

Factories, burning
with orange smoke, cut
steel plates with blue
arcs, welders patch up
the weapons
of war

dream.

> . . . und die sechzehn runden Säbel,
> die auf ihn zuspringen, Strahl um Strahl,
> sind ein Fest.
> Eine lachende Wasserkunst.

The Seaman

Near the seashore's changing arc, sands
slip back, tides push against the
land a bobbing shape, bluedenimed shoulders
humped, derelict, laced with foam, his face
pounds on bottom coral

                    —eyes of coral, webbed
& split by salt he arrives messenger
of no known ship, a calling
left before sea

          Above sirens
thudding bare feet rush to rescue
what cannot be saved, the sea's low rolls
lift the husky body, the pale hands push
against the sand & the chipped, the wrinkled
eyes, head rising, the eyes of a sailor
look last to the landbound men

& I
who no longer go to sea,
turn away, turn
away, the sounds of sea
at my back, turn, turn
away.

The Hanging Of Billy Budd

the quick
                —jerk

i

what would a man
see if his eyes
were not blindfold?

the stretching sea?

a wake bubbling
blue, behind the gulls
a darkness?

a young face
halfshut eyes
looking out

what would they
see?

ii

an innocence

        (no thing
    stands as innocent as the
sea, knowing no
    wrongs, a simple
        power

in one man
the flash of a knife
awakens, dark thunders

all men perhaps facing the
same in this fierce
excitement

and at a man's
own death?

a rough tickle
about the neck, wind
kicking at the hair
high above, looking
down

what would he see
but the easy pitching
ship, the pale faces
the watch, assembled
below

an innocent sea
calm as God's eyes

The Bridge, the Sea

At night, the LST bucking low waves
moon ten degrees on the port quarter, a following
wind and the crew sleeping below.

        The open bridge
overhangs the sea, waves slapping bow, the engines
vibrate, tickle, reassure the palm of the resting hand.

Of all watches, the mid is longest. OOD's love it,
fear it: in those grave endings of the night the sea
is spokesman, a gay killer who must be watched
because of his charms . . .

      sea, sea gods dancing
in the green, green eye . . . the crew sleeps on
below, engines push a phosphorescent wake
into darkness.

Ballad Of A Sailor

> . . . *wave,*
> *interminably flowing*
> —Wallace Stevens

It is because my fingers
move over these keys
compulsively
that the result
> *quiets me*

Dark images of war,
storms, hands raised like waves
in my dreams the wind
never stops

betrayed shores
sick girls in foreign bars
children begging outside
a night that is always closed

Comrades, their drowning faces
pale tourmaline, rayed with light,
open eyes and seawashed mouths

It is because my fingers
move over these keys
restlessly
that the chanty
> *moves me*

Here, far from the sea,
this house is steady. It does
not rock and that noise is
thunder, not gunfire. It is
peaceful here. Say it again.
Peaceful. One has only to stay
awake, not dream, the faces of dreams

cannot touch, dreamed blood stains
only the bedsheet sails of haunted ships.

Sailing, sail on, its crew of phantoms
wave, passing beyond the light, wave
& giggle among the shrouds, knowing
it is not the last goodbye nor the first
we are sharing.

the ex-officer, navy

the man, in whose eyes gunfire
is a memory, a restless dream
of stuttering mouths, bright flame

a man, who no matter how long the days
faces still the combat, the long night's terror—

> beyond the shoreline, gray muzzles train,
> the destroyer's bow breaks cleanly, all mounts
> at ready, general quarters: racing feet
> grunting rasping horn. tight stomach.
> knotted muscles in the shoulder, neck.

on white bare feet, with flaring eyes he greets
the morning, peace—advancing age. the dead faces once
again firm, smiling, ready for battle fade
gray smoke against a city's sun.

MidWatch

—Captain, from his quarterdeck

I would only wish you
happiness

    & yet I rage
& lunge against the night, cry
a name not yours, speak the terrible
words She gave me, put upon my lips
this strange song

Here, with the darkness like chains
about me, I dream of you, would touch
your breast, put my head beside yours—

Know that. I give courses for others,
lay out tracks on snowy, fresh charts
& all the while I am in the grip
of a current that sweeps me along
through the gutting rock & the seabird's
harsh cries

    From wherever I am I only wish you
love & take another turn about the deck
of this cramped room, this turning street.
We are not always what we say we are.
I, not always what I would be, for you.

Yet, here, caught now in this midnight
madness, seeing with more clarity than
this lamp should allow, I know I follow
another, Her thin hair caught to an
Easterning breeze, sudden gusts to catch
Her silver hair & lash it out like snakes
while the wood groans & cries in Her
voice about me. Seahag, figurehead of the
dark nightwatches the new moon catches
Her bony back & I must follow in the hollowed

shadows of Her eyes, the wrecking coasts,
the torn skies flapping like sail
canvas, the ruinous cries of birds
& broken bells. . .

I would wish you somewhere else
than here, some other love than mine.
And take my turn beside the wheel.

SeaDream

Before this light
what eyes, but mine,
were caught to this color?

dark waves, foam
colored to froth
bones, bones
ride darkgreen crests

       —ghosts, thin
faces
    a wave here
there, a destiny sails
beyond a horizon always

beyond

      a color, changing
      to a new light

         ii

Old men
who stand
beside the sea

. . . fading eyes,
leaning on canes

crippled gulls
fighting the blue
crying, they disappear

iii

bright, bright sails!

Endlessly sailing ships
setting forever courses, taff-rail
logs cutting their thin wakes:

> *a sun, going*
> *copper, brightly*
> *lighted, the figure head*
> *a young firm girl*
> *with a seashattered*
> *face*

golden gulls, crying
"Death!" as they swoop
Eastward the night
opens its black rose

Seacaptain

I never belonged to you.

Always the wind blew clean
& fresh to my face.

My friends are deadvoices.
My loves, the seas breaking
upon discarded conchshells.

I never belonged
but heard always

deadmouths crying through the fog
touched coolsteel at night, salt
winds rising, and far away
the buck & heave of a nunbuoy's bell.

I never. I'm sorry.
I listened always.
The seacrystals of my breath
& the rigging stiffbearded with ice,
seawinds that no longer call a specific name.

The world, hulled down, glistens
disappears with the horizon, night
closing behind the darkening wake.

Seachanty: Burial Song

blow the man down, laddies, blow
the man
down . . .

And speak over his bier the songs
spent in ancient time hauling
a capstan winch or shouted
drunk to the bars of the world.

Let friendship be a passing
sealight, which promised safety
while we sailed on to the next port.

Burn his candles low, since we
are paying for them and instead
of dust, cast salt, seasalt
—that's important. Let every man
know that here's a sailor and we
loved him. He should be buried
at sea, there's the thing, don't
you know? But he died ashore.
So sprinkle a little salt on him
that he'll know he's home once more.

Chorus

the wind howls past
the saltspun bar, the reef
with its screaming seabirds

and strange is the port
we come to, the girls
with dried lips and gusty
eyes to meet us, sailors,
come from the seas

so let no man blow you down,
laddie, let no man get your windward . . .

I speak to you not of oceans
but of the desperate time I've had
making you understand.

It's a strange world
and whether you sail
upon the seas or walk
hatless and supperless
on the land, the great waves
of sky break above you.

You have heard the sea
bird's cried dream. The taste
of longing before your eyes
grew dark watching the circling
fish, the green, green water
bubbles following you down
to the sand where you kissed
and the grains stuck to your lips.

no man blew you down, laddie.
it was the nature of the papers you signed,
the cargo of your voyage.

Somewhere In Washington, In Rome

Somewhere in Washington, in Rome,
the War Office in Bucharest, in Sofia,
Moscow

      —in the great cities of Europe
and America, there is The Book.
I have always imagined it black
calf's leather with heavy gold letters:

    GRAVES REGISTRY

(By now of course each book is fat
swollen with its names and places.
Gigantic, the one in Washington
would bulge the largest room, still
growing hourly with the dead and lost
of the country. Their names, insofar
as each could be identified. Next
of Kin, if any. The nature of the death,
when known.)

Murdered civilians and the enemy
are not there. Only those who died
in battle or later, in their beds,
their brains burning to the old gunfire
as they faced their last edged night.

He dies, his name appears instantly
within The Book comes a whirring a click
and ink blossoms on the appropriate page.
The Book then waits.

StarChart

Bending my already stiff fingers
to the words & signs I can catch,
following to the limits of my ability
that which I, and I alone, can sieze
hold

        —still I know some starship
will arrive, burst casually forth
with poems

        Crystals held in the hand!
        Activated by one's own energy!
        Triggering brainresponses
        without words! A high singing
        of the bones!

Poems greater than those I hear
but cannot yet, even granted the limits
of a medium heavy with printed pages,
speak

We are only men
gesturing in the fog & smoke
of time past & time to come

We,
sailing from one charted dot
to another, the whole planet
hurtling through unmapped space.

Summer Meadows

—for Aurel Rău

When I was a boy
the sounds of summer
opened my ears

before my eyes
caught their first light.

Meadowlarks and crows.

That's how I would describe
my life then, with snakes
thrown in for good measure.

Crows have bright eyes.
I never looked at meadowlarks'.

The tongue of a snake is gentle
to the skin, probing, without rancor
it explored the possibilities of my hands

then he slipped off into the fresh grass
of morning, his skin, it made a song
rustling off my hand.

Transylvanian Set Piece

As if there were not enough beauty in the world
there had to come Carpathian summers.
The high green meadows with the birds, the dresses
peasant girls on their ways to church and love.

The hammering of the monk at the biserica, whispers
of the devout from deep incense caves within
the springtime past, the mellowness of July without
blemish the days flow by as they have always done,
swift roses caught in brilliant nights, history
always attendant upon this maid holding her ardent
face to a light it would not have without this memory
of centuries spent about this church, girls dressed
in these very same dresses, hundreds of years dead,
yet walking in summertime mountain dreams of love.

Gypsy Bears

—In a dream of night
frost crystals on the tips of furs
capture the face of a dark girl,
a ring of golden gypsy furs, her eyes
wait in a cold that dances

With bears to carry the moon away
on their graceful shoulders

The Minaret At Constanta

I had always said I lived here
before but the proofs hid in the mists
of brain, clouded, unsure . . .

        We were camped
at Mamaia, the Romania resort on the Black Sea,
and, after settling in among the Poles and Czechs,
one day the children asked to see the city.

We loaded into the VW bus and drove until
the slim blue spire of the only minaret left
in all Romania caught the children's attention
and there we went.

            Well, I am an older man now
and 450 steps were a bit much for me, but I did it,
stood heaving but victorious at the top.
Among all the Romania tourists we Americans
stood out but they all smiled at me, so out
of shape I could not enjoy the view. Slowly
I raised my head

            saw the gate I had dreamed of
since childhood, without understanding, encrusted
with lions, in front of the palace, a toy Balkan house
nearly in ruins and one second I was a middle-aged
American, the next a slim, dark man in evening clothes
inside a coach, looking at that place when it was new,
candles lighting the window in welcome for me.

I start to get out, knowing I am going to have dinner
there, to see her, and then I am back to the American.
I shudder with the flash of time and say,

            "We must go to the Casino.
            I spent much time there."

76

My wife and children looking with such strange eyes
as I led them through Constanta's twisted and long
loved streets, straight as a dove flies I led them
to the miniature Monte Carlo that still sits
on a jetty out into the Black Sea and once again

I sat on that terrace, drank cognac in reverence
for whatever that night long ago might have meant
to that me who lived a little while ago and remembered
so long a night, candles, her lips, and lions.

The Casino At Constanta

Here is where that I stood.
Its hand upon this railing,
cigarette in hand thinking
of a woman, fingers, candlelight.

The music drifted across the sea.
I had had dinner at the House of Lions.
I passed through these gates, cognac

still on my lips. I crush stone
with my cigarette, turn my back
to the night, stirring with secrets.

Now is another year. The waiters'
grandsons no longer recognize me.
This suit is not the fit I knew.

Strange how sunlight dissolves
ghosts, yet leaves their scent.
I know who she was that night.
She, whose eyes were brighter than the sea.

1894-1974

A Prayer For Rivers

I live in the twilight of my vices,
old winds that blow across my face.

I know the stillness of the night.
I walk, the rivers are bright with moon.
Wrapping my coat about my neck, I pray,
to whatever gods, that night leaves me
not alone, but full, drifting down this street,
this time, you completely beside me,
riverfrost on your hair, and on mine.

—Somesh River, Romania

Love Motif: A Girl's Song

In counterpoint, I balance. I contrive.
All that I have come to expect, fades,
yet I balance, again, the same foolish line,
smile the same smile

                    knowing as a rock does
the gentleness of time, the soft wearing away.

I, she said, would sing this song.
I would know the cold sleet, the rain.
I raise my head through this rain
to look at you, windswept evening, your
face caught to raindrops, roar of the river.

How to speak of your eyes, here,
exactly at the center of the night?

One Rose Of Stone

Carved out of granite.

How can anyone believe that
or understand the patience
that caused a pair of hands
to painfully shape this flower
so perfectly, so carefully
then place this stone rose here
on this grave, just to mark a love?

The Celt In Me

In a museum here I saw a Celtic swordblade,
rusted, bent in combat. No handle.
These men who built what now are shadowed ruins,

my ancestors: from deathmasks, carvings
I see similar features. Gaiety, defiance,
Lost causes, futile wars. Indians of Europe.

Always the High Goddess, Moon Lady of White
streaming with light with eyes that touch
as the breeze moves through the Holy Tree.

From ancient barrows, dim men with old robes
walk gravely through the Danube mists
their arms outstretched for me.

—Dej, Romania

Child's Tale

I know a story
he said.
A wolf ate me.

And that
was the end
I asked?

No,
he said,
I became a rock

and the wolf
he died instead.
You can see him
in my eyes, he said.

—Snagov, Romania

Seadream

Romania is too much a part of me,
of nightgulls that sweep
the Black Sea and cry about
the breakwaters of Constanta.

Queen Marie was right.
No one can resist the love
these hills bring to darkly
touch your face and seek
the centered marrows of your bones.

Light has a peculiar quality here.
Fingers brush your face as you sleep.
There are pipes in the hills, and bears,
Great bears that walk the seas in moonlight.

The Undead

He who walks out of history, the clouds
of mourning about him. Could it be
that the legends of these Danubian fields,
the woods darkened by the blood of years
all conceal a common but feared truth?

None of us really die but merely walk on,
bones and flesh left uneasily, behind
us, all that awareness of where we've been
—what we have seen darken the moons
choke the Spring streams of lands
we never visited, in his life.

Does not the Bloody Count walk within
each of us? Seeking always life untouched,
the bare throat of love, our gaze caught to a fire
or these shepherds on a hillside in Moldova,
the high clear call of a fluted dream.

                  —Snagov, Romania
                    The Monastery
                    Where He Lies in His Tomb
                    They Say

Hebrew Stones

—near the Russian Border

At this village close to the North
we all stand quietly before a black stone.
"Here," it says in Hebrew, "are buried 50 persons.
They were murdered by the water."

June 15, 1941

Fifty yards away flows the swift stream.
On a headstone just beyond, the name "Wasserman,"
and I think of my friends of the same name,
Waterman, they were from near here, their family.

How gently the stream moves,
young leaves of spring floating
twisting down, flashing silver coins,
beside the old gravestones of Hebrews
as they sink slowly into rich earth,
grass and early flowers rustling
to a cool breeze, blowing from Russia.

Tunnel Mountain Campground

—Banff, Alberta
August 12, 1984

Trying to sleep, 11 p.m., the dust and rain of 4000 miles
all around me now, Heloise sleeping, her
soft breathing, the small noises of the camp settling down.
I am waiting, somehow I know that.

Suddenly I hear them—coyotes, the high shrillness
the fierce yelpings. I can sense them, fanned out
on the Western rim of the campground, halfway up the slope,
cacophony of pure noise, telling the small creatures
they are coming in the joy of darkness and chase.

Finally they stopped and his singing began, soft,
rising as the moon rose, shone through my tent flap,
heya, heya, heyo! Another hunting song I thought, about
the old days my father told of before there were roads
or campgrounds torn out of the living night by Coleman flares

heya, heya, heyo, heyo . . . .

No, he was singing an evening song, saying he was here,
honoring the old beliefs, mourning the passage of ways
that held earth as beloved body of mother, all creatures
much the same to Her who nurtured all, Her bleeding body,
my eyes closing to his pain as the beating heart of mountain
became his drum, as ravens carried the night away,
holding his song, his song

—for Ted Enslin

Chantey

I have taught most of my life, naval officer
dreams, the spit of guns aside, I have really
passed most of my working hours dueling with
words and minds, raised a good family, done what
ever I thought needed the doing—

        "Always at sea, I was slow. . . ."

knew Rilke better than the Atlantic, yet loved
the sense of the rudder, the hang of a tiller
just as I put about, red and green lights
marking the harbor's call as we dodged ships,
big and small. . .

I have spoken of the way the desert resembles
the sea, but what can substitute for the salt wind,
the gull's cry?

I watch the eyes of my students, see the gleam
of coastlines through my binoculars, live here
know that my desert is a condition of soul,
not topography. It is where one wrestles with devils
and knows they are oneself. It is so clear out here,
where the light is not muddy, but fierce as angel's
eyes, with the mountains to remind us of our frailties.

Southwestern Calvacade: A Postscript

I leave here, never leaving
at all. Come back, eager
for the death haunting a land
where I was born

—am most familiar with ghosts
   now they move by name
   across dreams I cannot

   stop them from moving, dancers
   in buffalo hides, grim faces
   under rusting helmets

I come back each time.
There are crows flying the fields
the scent of rain across the desert
& in the hollow cones of lava mountains
—a darkness beyond the sun.

The dead, they cut heavy trails
here. Their dust upon our boots
we walk these old, old Ways.

The cover illustration and book design is by
Vicki Trego Hill of El Paso, Texas.

The type is Clearface and is set by
Business Graphics of Albuquerque, New Mexico.

The book is printed by
Thomson-Shore of Dexter, Michigan.

EL PASO • TEXAS

Las Cruces, N.M